FROM POWER TO TYRANNY

Unveiling the Dark Secrets of the Throne

Robert A. Brooks

Copyright © 2023 Robert A. Brooks

All rights reserved.

No part of this publication may be reproduced, distributed, or transmitted in any form or by any means, including photocopying, recording, or other electronic or mechanical methods, without the prior written permission of the publisher, except in the case of brief quotations embodied in critical reviews and certain other noncommercial uses permitted by copyright law.

Table of Contents

INTRODUCTION

In a mysterious and secretive kingdom, a young historian named

Janet found an old diary hidden in the royal archives. The diary had important information that could reveal the secrets of the throne. It told a story about how people in power were doing bad things and this was a danger to the whole kingdom.

As Janet read more of the diary, she found out about a time long ago when King Richard was in charge. At first, he was a fair leader, but he gradually became a cruel and ambitious ruler. This story tells about a ruler who was once powerful but then lost his power. It shows how he did things secretly to betray the trust of the people who believed in him

As Janet continued reading, she became more and more curious. She couldn't shake off the disturbing parts of the book that talked about lies, betrayal, and the relentless quest for power. She was determined to find the truth, so she started a dangerous journey through dangerous places and met mysterious people who had parts of the answer.

As Janet was going, she met someone unexpected who became her friend. This person, named Marcus, was very wise and knew a lot about the history of the kingdom. They worked together to solve the mysterious clues in the diary, figuring out the lies that had trapped the throne. They went on a mission and went through hidden rooms, secret pathways, and forbidden halls. They encountered danger at every turn and were very close to making a big discovery.

Janet and Marcus discovered that the hidden truths about the throne were not only from the past but also had an impact on the present. The kingdom still felt the effects of a cruel ruler, and if they didn't stop it, they could make the same mistakes again.

Janet and Marcus wanted to bring fairness and make things equal. They gathered the people who were being treated badly and gave them hope. But with the bad people getting closer, it was a rush to find out the truth and stop the same thing from happening again.

Janet was stuck between being loyal to someone or finding out the truth. She knew that if she exposed the secrets of the throne, it would have serious consequences. However, with bravery, strong will, and a strong wish for fairness, she promised to expose the long-lasting troubles that had been affecting the kingdom.

"From Power to Tyranny: Revealing Secrets of the Throne" is an exciting story that will bring readers on an interesting adventure of surprises, deceit, and finding forgiveness. As we learn more, readers will wonder about the real power of rulers and the careful balance between their responsibilities and the vulnerability of the people they rule over.

CHAPTER 1: THE RISE OF POWER

JOURNEY OF AN AMBITIOUS INDIVIDUAL AIMING FOR THE HIGHEST POSITION OF POWER

In the bustling city of Veridia, amidst individuals filled with ambition and grand aspirations, resided a youthful individual known as Alexander Sinclair. Since he was young, Alexander was fascinated by the idea of having power and control over others. He had a strong desire to reach the top position of authority and was never satisfied with what he had. He had big dreams and wanted to change the world to be exactly how he wanted it.

With intelligence and cleverness, Alexander started a determined journey to achieve his big goal. He learned about diplomacy by watching how powerful people talked to each other and analyzing their strategies. He spent a lot of time studying history, learning about the plans and actions used by successful leaders who had achieved the highest level of power.

However, Alexander faced several obstacles along his way. He met other people who wanted the same powerful job as him and were just as determined to get it. He faced tough competition every day, which made him tough and made him change how he did things.

Despite facing setbacks, Alexander understood the significance of building relationships and alliances. He went to many parties and gatherings, easily figuring out the complicated plans of politics. He used his charm to win over important people in Veridia, gaining their trust and building a group of loyal followers.

But as Alexander went higher and got closer to his main goal, he started to understand the negative outcomes of his strong desire. Friendships became alliances that were only useful for the moment, and trust was not really there. As he gained more power, he got involved in a complicated situation where he had to make hard decisions that went against his own values.

Feeling guilty about the decisions he made, Alexander found comfort in thinking about himself and his actions. He wondered if the cost of achieving power was worth the things he gave up during his journey. Was he ready to give up his honesty and abandon his real beliefs to become king.

Alexander was torn between wanting to be powerful and wanting to leave a lasting impact. The trip that used to give him energy now made him feel very burdened.

As he looked at the city he wanted to be in charge of, Alexander started to understand the real price of wanting too much and not being controlled. He saw the pain of people who had been harmed by dishonest leaders. He heard their pleas for fairness loud and clear, and it made him feel a deep understanding and sympathy.

Alexander made a very important decision that would change his life. Instead of selfishly seeking power, he decided to commit himself to improving Veridia and its people. He understood that being truly great didn't depend on having a high position or power, but on making a positive difference in other people's lives.

With a new goal in mind, Alexander's journey took a surprising turn. He focused his ambition on creating a fair society, using his power to tackle unfairness and working hard to make opportunities available to everyone. His change inspired the people nearby, as his goal of becoming powerful turned into a noble mission for the benefit of everyone.

"Exploring the Journey of Ambition: From Power to Purpose" is a story that looks closely at why people want power and how they can change and become better. This text is saying that self-reflection can lead to change and it shows that true greatness is not based on our position in life, but on the positive impact we have on others.

INITIAL MOTIVATIONS AND ACTIONS TAKEN TO CLIMB THE LADDER OF AUTHORITHY

To climb the step of specialist, it is vital to have a clear beginning inspiration and take vital activities. The introductory inspiration to climb the stepping stool of specialist frequently emerges from a crave for individual development, career headway, expanded impact, and the opportunity to form a more prominent affect in an organization or industry. Here are a few key actions that people regularly take to attain this objective:

1. Self-Assessment: The primary step is to evaluate one's aptitudes, qualities, shortcomings, and regions for advancement. This contemplative handle makes a difference recognize the vital competencies required for higher-level parts.

2. Goal Setting: Setting up clear and achievable objectives is basic. These objectives ought to adjust with one's long-term vision and aspirations. Setting turning points and timeframes will offer assistance in following advance and remaining centered.

3. Continuous Learning: Committing to deep rooted learning is fundamental. Taking courses, going to workshops, seeking after progressed degrees, or obtaining modern certifications are ways to upgrade information and abilities in particular ranges of intrigued or mastery.

4. Grow Network: Building a solid proficient arrange is fundamental for career progression. Locks in in industry occasions, joining significant affiliations, going to conferences, and organizing with colleagues and coaches can provide get to to profitable openings, direction, and recommendations.

5. Proactive Approach: Rather than holding up for openings to emerge, people ought to effectively look for them. This will include taking on modern challenges, volunteering for ventures, or communicating intrigued in higher-level duties. Illustrating activity and an eagerness to require on extra duties can draw in the consideration of administrators and decision-makers.

6. Develop Leadership Skills: Building solid authority abilities is vital when yearning for higher positions. This incorporates creating compelling communication, decision-making, problem-solving, and team-building capacities. Looking for authority openings inside the organization, volunteering for authority parts in community or industry organizations, or serving as guides can offer assistance hone these aptitudes.

7. Seek Feedback and Mentorship: Effectively looking for criticism from administrators, colleagues, and coaches can give profitable bits of knowledge into zones that require change and offer assistance in individual advancement. Additionally, looking for out coaches who have effectively climbed the stepping stool of specialist can give direction, bolster, and important bits of knowledge into exploring the way to higher-level parts.

8. Deliver Results: Reliably conveying high-quality work and surpassing desires is basic for picking up acknowledgment and climbing the step of specialist. Going over and past in one's current part will help set up a solid notoriety and increment the likelihood of being considered for progression openings.

9. Adaptability and Resilience: The travel to climb the stepping stool of specialist frequently comes with challenges and misfortunes. People ought to illustrate versatility, versatility, and the capacity to memorize from disappointments. Remaining diligent and keeping up a positive attitude is pivotal within the confront of impediments.

10. Personal Branding: Showing oneself as a valid and profitable proficient is critical for career headway. This includes building a solid individual brand through reliably illustrating ability, conveying on guarantees, and setting up a notoriety as a solid and dependable person.

CHAPTER 2: THE SEDUCTION OF POWER

HOW THE ALLURE OF POWER BEGINS TO CORRUPT THE PROTAGONIST'S MORALS AND DECISION MAKING

In multiple tales, the main character's longing for power can result in their corruption and the adoption of poor judgment. This change usually happens slowly, influenced by a mix of things we want and things that others want us to do. When the main character starts to be attracted to the advantages and control that power provides, their original goals and beliefs may begin to weaken.

At first, the main character might think that having power can help them reach good goals or make the world better. However, when someone has a lot of power, they may feel tempted to go against their own beliefs and make choices that might not be morally right. They might do things that they used to think were wrong or bad, but now they think these choices are necessary for the benefit of many people or themselves.

When the main character becomes stronger, they might discover new chances and options that were not available before. This experience can be tempting, making you want more power and control. The desire for power becomes never-ending, making it hard to tell what is right and wrong. This causes the main character to focus more on their own interests than caring about other's well-being.

The attraction of having power can make the main character feel like they are invincible. They might come to think that the rules don't apply to them anymore or that they can't be criticized. This pride makes them lose sight of what is right, and they become less aware of the outcomes of what they do.

Over time, the main character's ability to make good choices becomes confusing because they want power so much. They might use tricks, lies, and even hurting others to keep their power or get rid of people that could be a problem. The main character's original set of morals becomes outdated as they give in to the negative effects of having power.

This wrongdoing often causes terrible outcomes for the main character and the people close to them. Relationships fall apart, trust is broken, and the main character's good intentions are completely overshadowed by their desire for power. In simple words: The protagonist becomes a morally corrupt person because of their desire for power. This shows that ambition can be destructive and dangerous if not controlled.

This story teaches us a lesson about the dangers of having too much power and the need to always stay true to our values, even when we are tempted to do otherwise.

THE GRADUAL SHIFT IN THEIR BEHAVIOR AND MOTIVATIONS BEHIND THEIR ACTIONS

The progressive move in behavior alludes to the recognizable and regularly unobtrusive changes in someone's activities, choices, and states of mind over time. It can be affected by different variables, counting individual encounters, outside occasions, and advancing viewpoints. Understanding the inspiration behind such behavioral shifts is basic in unraveling the reasons behind these changes.

Inspiration alludes to the fundamental driving constrain or reason behind an individual's activities or behavior. It can be categorized into inborn inspiration, which comes from inside oneself, and outward inspiration, which is affected by outside components. Looking at the inspiration behind someone's activities can give important experiences into their eagerly, needs, wants, and objectives.

To analyze the continuous move in behavior and the inspiration behind it, one ought to consider a few key components. These incorporate:

1. Individual Development and Improvement: People may experience behavioral changes as they develop, create, and pick up unused encounters. This could be driven by their want to investigate modern openings, extend their information, or look for individual fulfillment.

2. Social Impacts: Individuals are regularly affected by the behaviors and states of mind of those around them. Changes in behavior may result from a want to fit in, accommodate to social standards, or look for endorsement from others.

3. Life Transitions: Major life occasions or moves, such as beginning a unused work, getting hitched, or encountering a misfortune, can incite behavioral shifts. These changes may stem from the ought to adjust, adapt with unused circumstances, or reevaluate one's needs.

4. Changing Values and Convictions: Over time, people might reexamine their values and convictions, driving to shifts in behavior adjusted with their advancing worldview. This may be impacted by individual reflection, presentation to modern thoughts, or changes in social or social settings.

5. Motivating forces and Rewards: The inspiration behind behavior can moreover be formed by outside components, such as rewards, acknowledgment, or unmistakable benefits. Changes in behavior may happen when people see a potential pick up or are driven by motivating forces.

6. Individual Well-being and Satisfaction: Behavioral changes can happen when people look for to progress their well-being, accomplish individual fulfillment, or seek after a sense of reason. This will show as a move towards more beneficial propensities, expanded self-care, or a center on individual fulfillment.

Understanding the slow move in behavior and the inspiration behind it requires cautious perception, compassion, and open communication. It is significant to consider the special circumstances and person contrasts that contribute to these changes. By taking a all-encompassing approach to analyze behavior, we are able pick up important experiences into the inspirations that drive people's activities.

CHAPTER 3: MACHINATIONS AND MANIPULATIONS

INTRICATE WEB OF POLITICAL MACHINATIONS AND MANIPULATION SURROUNDING THE THRONE

When it comes to the complicated network of political schemes and manipulations, we step into a world where power struggles, strategic moves, and relentless pursuit of goals come together. These complicated systems are important in influencing how politics and governing works.

Political machinations are when people or groups plan and do things on purpose to gain power or control. These actions can include secretly persuading politicians, influencing public opinion through the media, making important connections, and using dishonest tactics to get ahead. To understand these actions, you need to carefully study the political system, the important people involved, and what drives them.

In politics, manipulations are different techniques used to control how people think, stop disagreement, or gain an advantage. Propaganda, misinformation, and spin are commonly used to influence what people think and to guide conversations in a specific way. Politicians can try to harm their opponents by spreading negative rumors about them, sharing secret information strategically, or using tricks to control how people feel and what they think.

In order to move around this complex situation, it is very important to understand the history of politics, beliefs, the social and political environment, and why different people do what they do. Understanding power dynamics, personal interests, and the hidden motives behind political strategies are important to uncovering the actions and intentions of individuals involved. Furthermore, by examining specific examples and noticing trends, we can gain useful understanding of the common tactics used in political scheming.

Analyzing political propaganda, verifying facts, and finding different sources of news can help to counter the manipulative methods used by politicians. When people participate in democratic processes like voting and keeping elected officials responsible, it helps to prevent political trickery.

Basically, understanding how politics work requires knowing how all the different parts work together. By studying the past, the way power is set up, and why people do things, we can understand the complicated world of politics and help make society more knowledgeable and alert.

THE VARIOUS TACTICS EMPLOYED BY BOTH THE PROTAGONIST AND THEIR RIVALS TO MAINTAIN OR SIEZE POWER

Within the complex scene of control flow, both heroes and their rivals utilize a wide range of strategies to preserve or seize control. These strategies can shift depending on the particular setting, but I will give an outline of a few common techniques utilized by both sides.

1. Influence and Control: One of the foremost predominant strategies utilized by heroes and their rivals is influence and control. They saddle the control of talk, publicity, and persuasive communication to shape open supposition, pick up bolster, and solidify control. This could include engaging to feelings, mutilating actualities, or misusing vulnerabilities of people or bunches.

2. Consolidation Building: Heroes and their rivals frequently lock in infusion building to accumulate partners and fortify their control base. They frame key organizations, manufacture collusions, and arrange bargains with powerful people or bunches to improve their political and social standing. By utilizing shared objectives and benefits, they make a organize of back that makes a difference keep up or grow their control.

3. Use of Force: In a few cases, protagonists and their rival's resort to constrain or the risk of drive to preserve or seize control. This could include military mediations, upsets, or rough concealment of restriction. The key utilizes of constrain points to dispose of or neutralize rivals and hinder challenges to their specialist.

4. Control of Resources: Control regularly lies in controlling key assets such as riches, normal assets, data, or key framework. Heroes and their rival's control or monopolize these assets to pick up impact and keep up their position. This may include financial methodologies like controlling markets, making restraining infrastructures, or controlling costs, as well as controlling data stream to shape open recognition.

5. Political Maneuvering: Heroes and their rivals lock in in complex political maneuvering to secure their control. This incorporates activities like locks in in policy-making, passing enactment, designating supporters to key positions, and utilizing political educate to solidify specialist. They explore the complexities of the political scene to outmaneuver rivals and keep up a favorable position.

6. Personal Charisma and Authority: The individual charisma and administration qualities of heroes can be instrumental in keeping up or seizing control. Charismatic pioneers motivate devotion and dedication from their supporters and are frequently gifted in open talking, captivating gatherings of people, and anticipating a solid picture of specialist. These qualities can offer assistance heroes rally supporters and counter the challenges of their rivals.

7. Covert Operations: Heroes and their rivals may lock in in incognito operations, such as surveillance, disrupt, or illegal exercises, to accumulate insights, debilitate adversaries, or destabilize existing control structures. These furtive strategies permit them to function watchfully and pick up an advantage over their rivals without drawing in open examination.

It is vital to note that the particular strategies utilized by heroes and their rivals incredibly depend on the setting, the nature of the control battle, and the assets accessible to each side. The flow can be affected by variables such as belief system, verifiable context, cultural standards, and the by and large adjust of control.

CHAPTER 4: THE THRONE'S SHADOW

UNCOVERS THE HIDDEN SECRES AND DARK PRACTICES THAT SUPPORT THE THRONE'S AUTHORITY

As an master in history and administration, I can give understanding into the flow that might support a throne's specialist, but I must clarify that I cannot give particular data approximately any specific position of authority or current occasions.

All through history, various positions of royalty have utilized strategies to preserve and solidify their specialist, a few of which have been disputable or considered dark. Here are a couple of cases of hones that have truly upheld the specialist of positions of royalty:

1. Propaganda and manipulation: Rulers have often utilized publicity to control open recognition and reinforce their authenticity. This will include controlling the account through censorship, advancing a particular picture of the ruler, and spreading deception to preserve their hold on control.

2. Observation and control: Numerous positions of royalty have depended on broad observation frameworks to screen citizens and stifle contradict. These hones can include mystery police strengths, covert sources, and intrusive reconnaissance advances to stifle restriction and recognize potential dangers to their specialist.

3. Political alliances and support systems: The throne's specialist can be strengthened by shaping vital unions with powerful people or groups. By dispersing assets, titles, and favors to steadfast supporters, the ruler can secure their loyalty and solidify control.

4. Suppression of contradict: Positions of authority frequently utilize strategies to quell any challenges to their specialist. This could include cruel measures such as detainment, torment, and indeed death of political rivals, blunt pundits, or restriction voices.

5. Co-opting devout educate: Generally, positions of royalty have forged alliances with devout teach to legitimize their run the show and fortify their specialist. By adjusting with devout figures, rulers have looked for to control or control devout stories to preserve open bolster and stifle disagree.

It is critical to note that these hones may not be all around appropriate and can shift depending on the authentic setting and locale. Furthermore, a few positions of authority or administering substances may have utilized diverse methodologies to preserve their specialist.

When people do shady things, they usually do sneaky or wrong activities to get an unfair advantage or hide what they are doing from the public. Shady dealings are when people do bad things with money such as lying about it, hiding it illegally, giving it to someone to get special treatment, trading stocks secretly, or doing other corrupt acts. These activities usually happen secretly to avoid getting into trouble with the law or harming one's reputation.

Dirty alliances are secret agreements or partnerships between people, groups, or countries that have bad intentions. These partnerships are often formed to benefit oneself or a group, without considering what is right or the happiness of others. These groups that work together often do illegal things and can include activities like organized crime, moving drugs around, smuggling weapons, or even manipulating political situations.

Illicit activities are actions that break the rules or laws that have been set. This group includes many different illegal activities, such as selling drugs, smuggling people, transporting illegal goods, committing computer crimes, making fake money or products, and selling illegal weapons. These activities are usually done secretly, out of the public's view, and are known for being hidden and potentially causing harm to society.

It's crucial to reveal and deal with these secret activities because they can weaken the legal system, create problems in economies, worsen inequality, and pose serious dangers to social and political stability. Governments, cops, and global organizations are important in looking into and punishing people involved in bad behavior, making sure they are responsible, and putting measures in place to stop and discourage such actions.

By exposing these secret and illegal activities, societies can aim for more honesty, fair behavior, and the protection of public welfare.

CHAPTER 5: SEEDS OF REBELLION

GROWING DISCONTENT AMONG THE OPPRESSED POPULACE AS A RESULT OF THE TYRANT'S REIGN

The complicated issue of the unhappiness of those subjected to a tyrannical ruler has many dimensions. When a mean ruler is in charge, they usually make unfair rules, stop people from expressing their opinions, and use scare tactics and force to stay in control. This makes people feel unhappy and frustrated, which causes different things to happen.

First, when a dictator is cruel, it can cause a lot of unfairness's in society, the economy, and politics. When a powerful ruler strengthens their control, they might make rules that benefit only a small group of people and ignore the needs and rights of most people. This makes people feel like things are unfair and makes them even more unhappy. It affects the people who are suffering the most from these policies.

Secondly, when a tyrant has power, they often prevent people from expressing themselves freely, gathering together, and enjoying other basic rights as humans. When people disagree or speak up against something, they are often punished in a harsh way, such as being put in jail, experiencing harm, or being scared. The oppressed people become even more unhappy because they don't have ways to peacefully express their opinions or have conversations with others.

Also, when a tyrant rules with harshness, people may start to lose faith in each other and their community. When people are always afraid and being watched, they become unsure about trusting others and making deep relationships. This can make society divided and prevent people from speaking up about their worries, which can make them feel alone and frustrated.

Additionally, the negative impact on the economy caused by a ruler with absolute power can worsen dissatisfaction. When people engage in dishonest activities, waste resources, and don't provide chances for the economy to improve, it can lead to many people being very poor, jobless, and treated unfairly. Financial difficulties, along with a harsh ruler who does not treat people fairly, can make the problems of an already suffering population even worse.

Over time, people becoming unhappy can show itself in different ways. People may protest, show their opinions, and disobey laws to make sure they are heard and to ask for change. People may form secret groups or organizations to challenge a ruler who oppresses them.

To summarize, when a ruler is oppressive, it leads to unhappiness and dissatisfaction among the people, which is a big result of having a dictator in power. The people are angry and frustrated because of rules that make them feel trapped, not being able to do what they want, how they are divided in society, and struggling with money problems. People often resist because they want freedom, fairness, and a better future for themselves and their communities.

INITIAL WHISPERS OF REBELLION AND THE SMALL ACTS OF RESISTANCE THAT BEGIN TO EMERGE

The first sign of rebellion usually starts when a group of people feel unhappy, oppressed, or treated unfairly in society. It can be a reaction to situations in politics, society, or the economy that are seen as not good or unfair. This soft voice is the first signs that people are starting to disagree with something. They express their frustrations and worries in private, talking to people they trust, like close friends or family.

As the rumors get louder, people start doing small things to resist. These actions are ways of showing resistance and opposition to the current systems of power. In the beginning, they might not seem important or easy to notice, but they can become powerful movements that make a big difference.

There are many ways to resist, even in small ways. They could involve secret meetings or gatherings where unhappy people get together to talk about their complaints and make plans for change. These secret meetings offer a way for people to come together and talk about their thoughts, understandings, and personal experiences. They help create a sense of unity among those who challenge the existing system.

Other ways to resist could include sharing different information or messages to make more people aware. This can be done by secretly publishing writings, drawing graffiti, or more commonly using online platforms. It allows people to question popular stories and share different points of view.

Additionally, when individuals choose not to comply with certain rules or laws, like engaging in civil disobedience or peaceful protests, it is a way for them to express their resistance. These actions can include things like refusing to buy certain products or not support certain organizations, as well as organizing peaceful gatherings, sitting inside a place or taking part in protests. By peacefully causing problems in how society works, these actions get people's attention and create energy for change.

It is when people start talking quietly and do small things against authority that the start of rebellion begins. This means that they are the first actions taken by people who want to challenge the way things are, ask why those in charge are making certain decisions, and work towards a better future. Over time, if these small acts of resistance become popular, they can turn into bigger movements, causing more important protests, revolutions, or major societal changes.

Throughout history, there have been many instances where small acts of rebellion and resistance have led to major changes. From standing up against colonial rule to fighting for equal rights and resisting oppressive governments, these first acts have the power to bring people together and change the course of history.

CHAPTER 6: THE IRON FIST

THE TYRANT'S TIGHTENING GRIP ON POWER AND THEIR USE OF BRUTAL FORCE TO MAINTAIN CONTROL

A cruel leader's increasing control over a country and their use of violent actions to stay in charge show how governance and human rights are getting worse. These accounts show a clear pattern of cruel tactics used by the ruler to silence disagreement, strengthen their power, and make people afraid.

One thing that is often seen in these stories is that democratic institutions are slowly being weakened and the system of checks and balances is being undermined. The mean ruler can change or take apart the existing rules, using ways to gain more power for themselves. This often means that they give themselves a lot of power, suppress other political parties that disagree with them, and control or weaken important parts of the government like the courts and the media.

Another important thing is the use of very strong physical force to stop people from disagreeing and to stay in charge. The ruler's government might use methods like controlling what people can say or see, watching them closely, and spreading misleading information to control how the public thinks and to stop anyone who disagrees. In very serious situations, this can lead to the unfair treatment, imprisonment, or killing of people who go against the ruler's power, like political enemies, reporters, or those who fight for human rights. These violent actions are meant to frighten others and make them too scared to oppose.

Additionally, these stories often show a group of loyal supporters and enforcers who help the ruler maintain their control over the country. This can mean creating a system where people are rewarded for being loyal and punished if they are not. The tyrant's closest allies and security team are very important in making sure that people obey his rules and stopping any protests or rebellions.

In simpler terms: In the end, the stories of a dictator's increasing control over power and their use of violent force show a frightening picture of a government that cares most about protecting itself. They are a strong reminder that being watchful, open, and protecting democratic values is necessary to prevent human rights violations and misuse of power.

CONSEQUENCES FACED BY THOSE WHO DARE TO CHALLENGE THE THRONE

When people set out to challenge the position of royalty, they regularly confront critical and far-reaching results. These results can change depending on the particular authentic, social, and political setting, but a few common results can be watched.

1. Loss of Power: Those who challenge the position of authority regularly put themselves in coordinate resistance to the administering specialist. This could result within the misfortune of any existing control or impact they may have held inside the current framework.

2. Political Persecution: Challenging the position of authority can lead to political mistreatment, where protesters are focused on, marginalized, or indeed subjected to viciousness. Rulers who feel debilitated by challenges to their specialist may utilize different strategies, counting detainment, banish, or indeed execution, to smother restriction.

3. Social Confinement: Challenging the position of royalty can regularly lead to social segregation and distance from companions, family, and the broader society. Supporters of the administering specialist may remove themselves from dissidents, driving to a misfortune of social status and back systems for those who challenged to challenge the position of authority.

4. Loss of Property and Wealth: Challenging the position of royalty may result within the seizure of property and riches. The administering specialist may seize the resources of dissenters as a implies to debilitate them financially and debilitate any advance restriction.

5. Historical Condemnation: In a few cases, those who challenge the position of authority may be condemned in verifiable accounts or by the administering authority. Their activities may be depicted contrarily, their thought processes addressed, and their bequest discolored. This will have long-lasting impacts on how they are recalled and seen in society.

6. Effect on Future Generations: Challenging the position of royalty can have results that amplify past the people straightforwardly included. Families and relatives of those who challenged to challenge the position of royalty may moreover confront segregation, disgrace, or proceeded marginalization, influencing their openings and social standing for eras to come.

It is vital to note that the results confronted by challengers can too be affected by components such as the administering regime's steadiness, the level of open back for the position of authority, and the strategies utilized by dissidents in their challenge.

CHAPTER 7: SHADOWS OF REDEMPTION

UNLIKELY HEROES WHO START TO PLOT THE DOWNFALL OF THE TYRANT

Let me introduce a group of different people who are united to
bring down a cruel ruler who is causing fear in their country. Every
person in this group is different and has their own skills and ideas.
When we work together, we become a strong force that can fight
against oppression and cannot be stopped.

First, we have Alex, who is very smart and great at planning. He
uses his intelligence and logical thinking to help the group. He is
really good at understanding how power works and knows a lot
about history. This makes him very important in helping to create
their plan.

Next is Zara, a talented and nimble thief who is well-known for her
skilled hands and ability to sneak into even the most heavily
protected places. She is very good at being sneaky and causing
trouble, which helps the group learn important information and
stop the bad leader's plans without making his loyal followers
aware.

Next, we have Malik, a person who used to serve in the military
and is a strong fighter. They are really good at fighting and always
believe in doing what is right. His strong commitment to defending
the innocent and overthrowing the oppressive ruler is a source of
motivation for everyone in the group.

Maya, a very skilled sorceress who uses powerful magic really
well, is also joining them. Her special powers are very helpful in

defeating the tyrant's powerful friends who also have special powers. Her powers also allow her to trick and surprise her enemies in unique ways.

Completing the group is Ravi, a charming trickster who is famous for his smooth talking and convincing abilities. Ravi is really good at understanding how people interact with each other and changing their opinions. He helps the group by making friends with people who could help us and making enemies become our friends.

Each person in this unusual group has their own weaknesses and fears, but these differences and vulnerabilities actually make them stronger together. They create a strong connection and give hope to the oppressed people. They also scare the tyrant and carefully plan to overthrow him.

Motivated by their strong longing for freedom, fairness, and equal treatment, this group of unexpected champions sets out on a brave and risky adventure, risking everything to free their country from the ruler's harsh and unfair rule and bring back calmness and success to their citizens.

MOTIVATIONS AND THE RISKS THEY ARE WILLING TO TAKE TO RESTORE JUSTICE AND FREEDOM

When people are propelled to reestablish equity and flexibility, their reasons can shift incredibly. Here are a few common inspirations and the dangers they may be willing to require:

1. Belief in fairness and correspondence: A few people are driven by a deep-rooted conviction within the significance of equity and equality for all. They may be willing to require critical dangers, counting individual give up and confronting restriction, to make a fairer society. This seem include challenging harsh frameworks, supporting for arrangement changes, or joining social developments.

2. Personal experiences of injustice: Individuals who have by and by experienced bad form may be propelled by their claim battles to battle for equity and opportunity. These encounters can fuel a solid crave to anticipate others from persevering comparative hardships. They may chance their security, notoriety, or individual assets to address the systemic issues that sustain bad form.

3. Moral or moral feelings: Inspirations driven by ethical or moral feelings include a solid sense of right and off-base. People willing to reestablish equity and flexibility based on these standards may be willing to require calculated dangers, indeed on the off chance that it implies going against societal standards or confronting backfire. They may winner causes in any case of the individual results, guided by their values and standards.

4. Commitment to social change: Some people are persuaded by a broader commitment to societal advance and changing existing control structures. They may be willing to require both individual and collective dangers, such as taking part in dissents, organizing grassroots developments, or locks in in respectful noncompliance.

Their inspiration stems from a want to challenge harsh frameworks and make enduring alter.

5. Sympathy and compassion: People persuaded by sympathy and sympathy look for to lighten the enduring of others. They may chance their claim security or consolation to ensure the rights and flexibilities of marginalized communities. These inspirations frequently include dynamic engagement in helpful endeavors, backing, or building steady systems to enable others.

It is imperative to note that each individual's level of risk-taking can shift based on their circumstances, individual values, and the particular setting in which they are working to reestablish equity and opportunity.

CHAPTER 8: THE FINAL SHOWDOWN

BUILDS UP TO THE CLIMATIC CONFRONTATION BETWEEN THE TYRANT AND THE REBELLION

A climactic encounter between a dictator and a resistance could be a key component in narrating that includes tension and escalated to the plot. Building up to this moment involves a few significant variables in arrange to form a captivating and impactful climax.

1. Establish the Tyrant: To begin with and preeminent, it is critical to set up the dictator as a impressive and forcing enemy. Create their character, inspirations, and activities in a way that exhibits their control and impact over the society or the characters inside the story. This makes a difference make a sense of criticalness and sets the arrange for the inevitable encounter.

2. Develop the Rebellion: The disobedience, on the other hand, ought to be depicted as an underdog battling against the tyrant's harsh run the show. Present the most characters who are portion of the resistance and emphasize their battles, inspirations, and individual stakes in contradicting the dictator. This makes a difference the group of onlookers ended up sincerely contributed in their cause and builds expectation for the climax.

3. Heighten Tensions: As the story advances, steadily heighten pressures between the dictator and the disobedience. Appear the tyrant's endeavors to smother or kill the disobedience, whereas moreover highlighting the rebellion's endeavors to accumulate back, arrange methodologies, and pick up energy. This back-and-forth battle increases the tension and keeps the group of onlookers locked in.

4. Foreshadow the Encounter: Drop clues or portend the inescapable encounter between the dictator and the disobedience all through the account. This could be done through typical symbolism, prophetic messages, or discourse between characters. Portending makes a sense of expectation, signaling that the extreme clash is drawing closer.

5. Increase Stakes: Raise the stakes as the story approaches the climax. Make the tyrant's activities harsher and annihilating, whereas moreover highlighting the potential results in the event that the resistance comes up short. This heightens the criticalness and reinforces the enthusiastic effect of the showdown.

6. Strategize and Plan: Grandstand the rebellion's vital arranging and preparation for the standoff. This seem include gathering partners, preparing their strengths, and concocting a intelligent technique to destroy or debilitate the tyrant's fortress. Including the gathering of people within the rebellion's arranging handle makes a sense of expectation and speculation in their victory.

7. Execute the Climactic Encounter: At long last, when the time comes, organize the climactic encounter between the dictator and the resistance. Make it the urgent minute of the story, where both sides confront off against each other with their full quality and assurance. Guarantee that the encounter is full of tension, activity, and emotional intensity, with the result essentially affecting the characters and the world they occupy.

ELEMENTS OF SUSPENSE, ACTION AND MORAL DELIMMAS AS THE FATE OF THE KINGDOM HANGS IN THE BALANCE

The kingdom of Eldoria, which is famous for being rich and peaceful, is facing a very important point in time because there is an unknown danger approaching its borders. Meet General Roland, a smart military planner who is famous for his strong determination and strong belief in fairness.

As the story goes on, it becomes clear that there is a secret group trying to take over the kingdom. This group is led by a person named Lucius who is both likable and questionable in terms of his morals. Their goal is to remove King Aldric from his position as ruler. Roland is conflicted because of his loyalty to the ruler, and he feels unsure about what to do when he discovers troubling facts about the kingdom's politics.

To create excitement, the rebellion keeps its actions a secret and takes place in the hidden parts of the kingdom. Roland is determined to find the truth, but he discovers a complicated situation involving lies, disloyalty, and giving up personal things that he has to handle. He is getting closer to the center of the plan with each step he takes, while time is running out and the kingdom is in danger.

The action scenes make the situation more urgent as Roland leads his loyal soldiers against Lucius's rebels. Intense fights break out all over Eldoria with exciting sword fights, powerful magic attacks, and risky face-to-face confrontations. These exciting moments not only show Roland's clever thinking but also represent the kingdom's struggle to stay alive.

Roland fights against Lucius and his rebellion. He is confronted with difficult choices that challenge who he is as a person and what he believes in. He realizes that things are not just simple and clear, but there are many complex aspects within the conflict. Roland is in a difficult situation because he has a responsibility to take care of the kingdom, but he is starting to question if King Aldric is ruling in a fair and just way. As he struggles with these moral problems, he has to make hard choices that might determine the future of the kingdom.

The future of the kingdom is very uncertain as Roland reveals a final, surprising truth that will change how power is divided in Eldoria. In a very suspenseful moment, he has to use his smart thinking, strong belief in fairness, and help from his loyal friends to make choices that will determine what happens to the kingdom.

Adding suspense, action, and moral problems to the story makes it more interesting and captivating. In the story, General Roland goes on a dangerous journey to rescue the kingdom, and readers enjoy following his adventures eagerly.

CHAPTER 9: THE AFTERMATH

CONSEQUENCES OF THE TYRANT'S DOWNFALL AND CHALLENGES FACED DURING THE TRANSITION TO A NEW ERA

The ruin of dictators can have far-reaching results, both positive and negative, which regularly come hand in hand with the challenges confronted amid the move to a modern time. Let's dig into these results and challenges:

1. Power Vacuum: When a dictator falls, it frequently clears out a control vacuum in their wake. This makes an opportunity for different groups or people to compete for control. The battle for control can lead to inner clashes, starting viciousness or gracious turmoil. The challenge here is to oversee this control vacuum and guarantee a smooth and tranquil move of specialist.

2. Political Turmoil: Within the consequence of a tyrant's ruin, there's ordinarily political turmoil as the existing control structures disintegrate. This may lead to a breakdown in administration, with frail or non-existent teach. Setting up unused political frameworks and structures gets to be a basic challenge, as the move requires exploring through complex political scenes and adjusting the interface of diverse groups.

3. Rebuilding Trust and Compromise: Beneath oppressive run the show, believe in educate, government, and indeed individual citizens tends to disintegrate. Modifying believe inside society gets to be vital to cultivate steadiness and solidarity amid the move. Moreover, accomplishing compromise between groups who were at chances amid the tyrant's run the show is challenging but fundamental for long-term peace and advance.

4. Financial Recovery: Oppressive administrations frequently prioritize their claim interface over the welfare of their country. Subsequently, their ruin can take off behind a battling economy with debilitated foundation and disturbed markets. Overcoming financial challenges gets to be a key perspective of transitioning to an unused period. This may include actualizing financial changes, pulling in ventures, and advancing work creation to revamp the economy and make strides the standard of living for the citizens.

5. Addressing Social and Humanitarian Issues: Oppression frequently brings almost social treacheries, human rights manhandle, and marginalized communities. Transitioning to a unused time requests tending to these issues, looking for equity for casualties, and executing arrangements that advance correspondence and inclusivity. It can be a complex challenge to guarantee a reasonable and fair society whereas tending to the grievances of the past.

6. International Relations: The drop of a dictator can to have suggestions for worldwide relations. The move to an unused time may require reshaping political ties, reassessing unions, and looking for acknowledgment from the worldwide community. Modifying believe and validity on the universal arrange is basic for cultivating participation, drawing in remote help, and joining into the worldwide community.

By and large, the results of a tyrant's ruin are multifaceted. Whereas it offers an opportunity for positive alter and advance, it too presents various challenges that must be explored carefully. Effective moves require visionary administration, comprehensive administration, viable institution-building, and a commitment to equity and compromise.

REFLECTS ON THE LESSONS LEARNED FROM THE ABUSE OF POWER AND THE POTENTIAL FOR A BRIGHTER FUTURE

It's important to think about what we've learned from people who have used their power in bad ways in order to make a better future for ourselves. In the past, we have seen many times when powerful people have used their power to benefit themselves, causing a lot of harm and suffering. However, we should also understand that these experiences have given society important knowledge and teachings to develop and change.

One of the biggest things we learn from people misusing their power is that we need to have a system in place to make sure they don't have too much control. Power should be spread out among many people or groups, because when only a few have power, they can easily misuse it. Instead, we need to put systems in place that make sure things are clear, people are held responsible, and those in charge can be held accountable for their actions. This can be done by having strong systems of government, a fair court system, freedom for newspapers and media, and involving citizens in making decisions.

Another thing we learn is how important it is to encourage leaders who make good choices and who follow their values when they have power. Leaders who focus on doing what is best for everyone and make choices with honesty, understanding, and treating others well are more likely to help make the future better. Training and education programs can help individuals develop the qualities needed to hold positions of power.

In addition, when people misuse their power, it shows how important it is to create a culture that values including and accepting a variety of people. When power is held by a group that is the same or similar, there is a greater chance of unfair treatment, keeping certain people out, and making others feel less important or valued. Promoting different viewpoints, diversity, and inclusivity is important because it makes power more equal and helps make decisions that benefit everyone in society.

In the end, when we see how power can be misused, we should be motivated to join in making a better future. We need to carefully watch over and defend the rights and freedoms of everyone, always questioning and fighting against unfair systems of power, and making sure others are responsible for their actions. By studying our past errors and aiming for a fair and equal society, we can make progress towards a better future where power is handled responsibly and the chance of mistreatment is reduced.

EPILOGUE: LEGACY AND LESSONS

REFLECTS ON THE LASTING IMPACT OF THE TYRANT'S RULE AND THE LESSONS THAT CAN BE DRAWN FROM THIS EXPERIENCE

The long-term effects of dictators' ruling are usually very strong and widespread. Their strict and controlling governments can cause long-lasting damage to societies, organizations, and people. One of the biggest effects is that people's basic rights and democratic principles are being taken away. Dictators usually create strict systems that take away the ability to speak freely, gather together, and express oneself. This effectively stops any disagreement or opposition and strengthens their control.

When there is a tyrannical ruler, people usually feel scared, threatened, and powerless. The way things are run and how fair decisions are made are weakened, which causes dishonesty, favoritism, and a lack of responsibility. Institutions like the courts, the press, and organizations in society are corrupted and work in favor of the people in power instead of doing what is fair and helpful for everyone.

Dictators also have a tendency to focus on getting richer and benefiting themselves instead of caring about the wellbeing of their people. The economy's resources are not being handled well, which causes a lot of inequality and poverty for most people. Meanwhile, a small group of privileged people get advantages from the government's policies. The differences between people's social and economic situations can last a long time even after the ruler's rule is over.

Furthermore, the effect on people's minds and the overall well-being of communities that experience cruel and oppressive governance is very deep. Fear, trauma, and a lack of trust in organizations and other people can last for many years. After a tyrant is no longer in power, it is important for societies to work on rebuilding trust, bringing people together, and creating a sense of justice and fairness. These are not easy tasks, but they are crucial for a society to move forward.

We can learn important lessons from the experience of tyrants ruling. First and most importantly, it is extremely important to protect and support democratic values, human rights, and the rule of law. Governments and societies need to actively protect these principles to stop the growth of authoritarianism.

Secondly, it is important to have strong and independent organizations in place to make sure that power is not abused or misused. Having a strong court system, independent media, and an engaged community are important for making leaders responsible and safeguarding people's rights.

Thirdly, it is very important to cultivate a society where people are involved in their communities, think carefully about issues, and actively take part in decision-making. This helps to prevent power from being concentrated in the hands of a small group of people. When people are well-informed and involved in their community, they can recognize and stand up against things that might harm democracy.

In short, it is important for all countries to help and encourage democracy and human rights around the world. Working together, helping each other, and sharing what we know and have can strengthen movements that support democracy and stop people with too much power from becoming rulers.

In simpler terms, the long-term effects of tyrants' rule are widespread and harmful. They impact not just organizations but also people and communities. The experiences taught us that it is very important to protect democratic values, make institutions strong, encourage people to participate in their community, and promote working together with other countries to defend human rights and democracy.

DEEPER UNDERSTANDING OF THE DELICATE BALANCE BETWEEN POWER, JUSTICE AND THE RESPONSIBILITY OF THOSE IN POSITIONS OF AUTHORITY

The long-term effects of tyrants' control are often deep and wide-reaching. Their cruel and controlling governments can cause lasting harm to societies, organizations, and people. One of the biggest effects is that our basic human rights and democratic principles are being slowly taken away. Tyrants usually create unfair systems that stop people from freely speaking, gathering, and expressing themselves, thus preventing disagreement and increasing their control.

When a ruler is tyrannical, the people usually feel very afraid, scared, and like they cannot do anything to help themselves. The way that laws are followed and how we run things fairly is weakened, causing corruption, favoritism, and a lack of taking responsibility for actions. Institutions like the courts, news outlets, and community organizations are controlled by the people in power and no longer work to support fairness and the well-being of the majority.

Dictators often put their own wealth and interests above the well-being of the people they rule. The government doesn't use money wisely, which makes a lot of people poor and unequal. But a small group of rich people benefit from the government's decisions. Social and economic differences can continue to exist for a long time even after a tyrant's rule has ended.

Additionally, the emotional and mental effects on people and communities who experience oppressive leadership are significant.

Fear, trauma, and losing trust in institutions and fellow citizens can last a long time, even for many generations. After a tyranny ends, it is very challenging for societies to regain trust, mend divisions, and create a fair and just system.

We learned some important lessons from the rule of tyrants. First of all, it is extremely important to protect and support democratic values, human rights, and the rule of law. Governments and societies need to stay watchful and protect these principles to stop authoritarianism from growing

Secondly, having strong and independent institutions is very important to make sure that no one person or group has too much power and that there is a fair system in place. A strong legal system, unbiased media, and involved community are very important in making sure leaders are responsible and protecting people's rights.

Third, it is important to encourage a culture where people are engaged in their community, think carefully about important issues, and actively take part. This helps prevent a small group of people from having too much control. A well-informed and involved group of citizens can work together to recognize and oppose dangers to democracy.

In short, it is important for all countries to help and encourage democracy and human rights everywhere in the world. When people work together, help each other, and share what they know and have, it can help democratic movements and stop cruel leaders from gaining power.

To put it simply, the long-term effect of tyrants' rule is widespread and harmful. It impacts not just organizations, but also people and communities. The important things we have learned from these experiences show that it is very important to support democratic values, make institutions stronger, encourage people to participate in their communities, and work together with other countries to protect human rights and democracy.

CHAPTER 10: CONCLUSION

"From Power to Tyranny: Unveiling the Dark Secret of the Throne" is an interesting exploration of how leaders can become tyrants. The book goes deep into the complicated way power works and shows the hidden truths and reasons behind the throne. In the book, the author skillfully talks about how people can be dishonest and use their power badly when they are attracted to being in charge.

The book tells a warning story about the bad things that happen when leaders only care about themselves and ignore the people they are supposed to be helping. It does this by doing a lot of research and telling interesting stories. The writer effectively explores past events, studies of politics, and understanding of the mind to reveal the negative side of leaders who have lost their way.

Moreover, the book "From Power to Tyranny" encourages readers to carefully analyze the way power works in today's society. This text tells us about the problems that can come up when one person or group has all the power. It also reminds us that it's important for leaders to be responsible, honest, and make good choices.

This book talks about how power can turn into tyranny, and it reveals hidden secrets and mechanisms that cause this. It is a thought-provoking and relevant contribution to the study of government, history, and how people behave. Readers gain a deep knowledge of how easily power can be lost and the duty that comes with attaining and keeping it.

In simple words, "From Power to Tyranny: Unveiling the Dark Secret of the Throne" is an interesting book that tells us about the importance of being watchful, standing up against mistreatment, and working together for a fair and right society.